Flower Designs and Pattern Coloring Book for Kids

I0485585

By
Adult Coloring Book J. Kaiwell
and
John Daniel

Published by PUBLISHING COMPANY in 2015
First edition: First printing
Illustrations and design © 2015 Author
allcoloringbook.com

All rights reserved. No part of this book may be reproduced or transmitted in any form or by any means, including but not limited to information storage and retrieval systems, electronic, mechanical, photocopy, recording, etc. without written permission from the copyright holder.
ISBN 978-1517124991

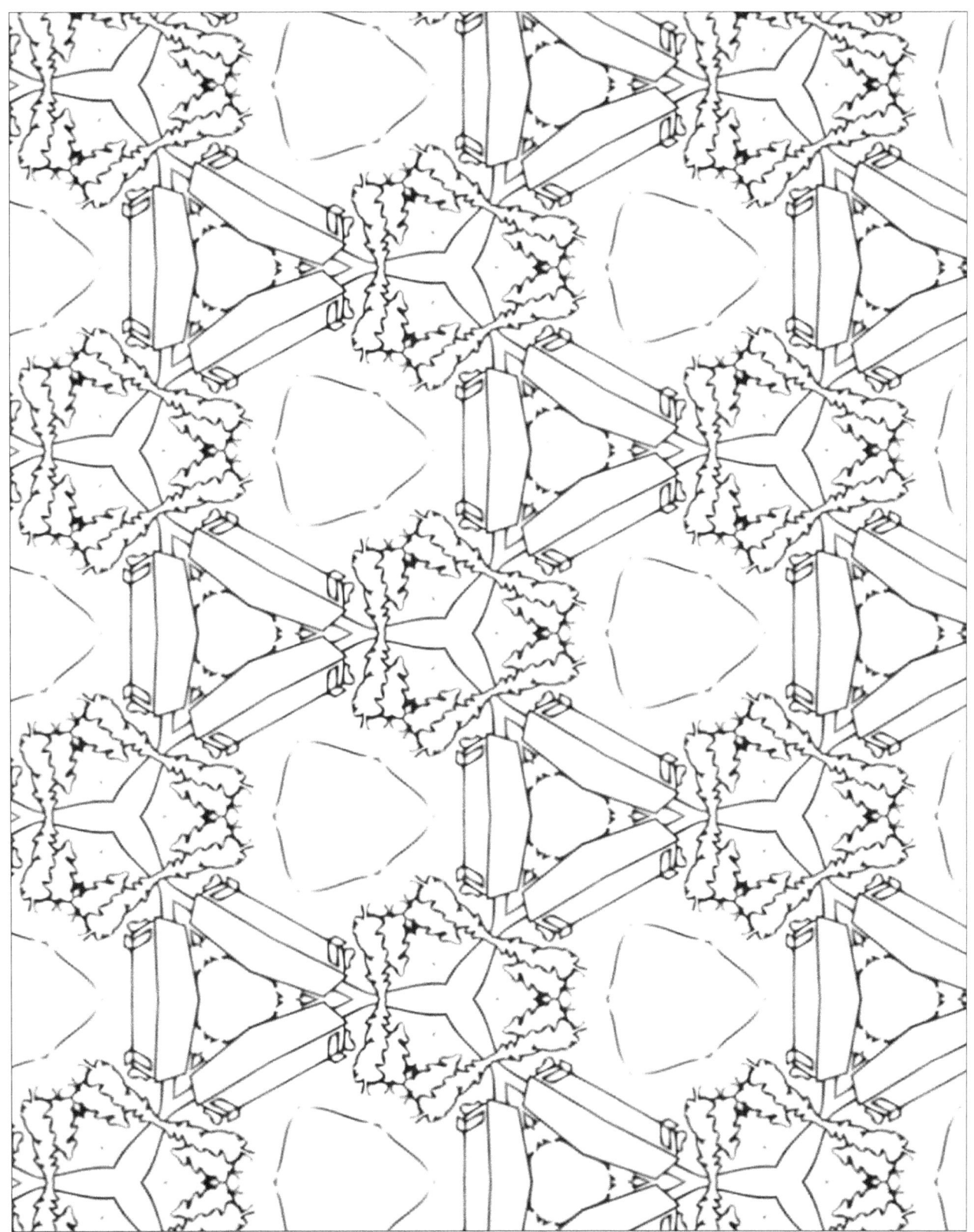

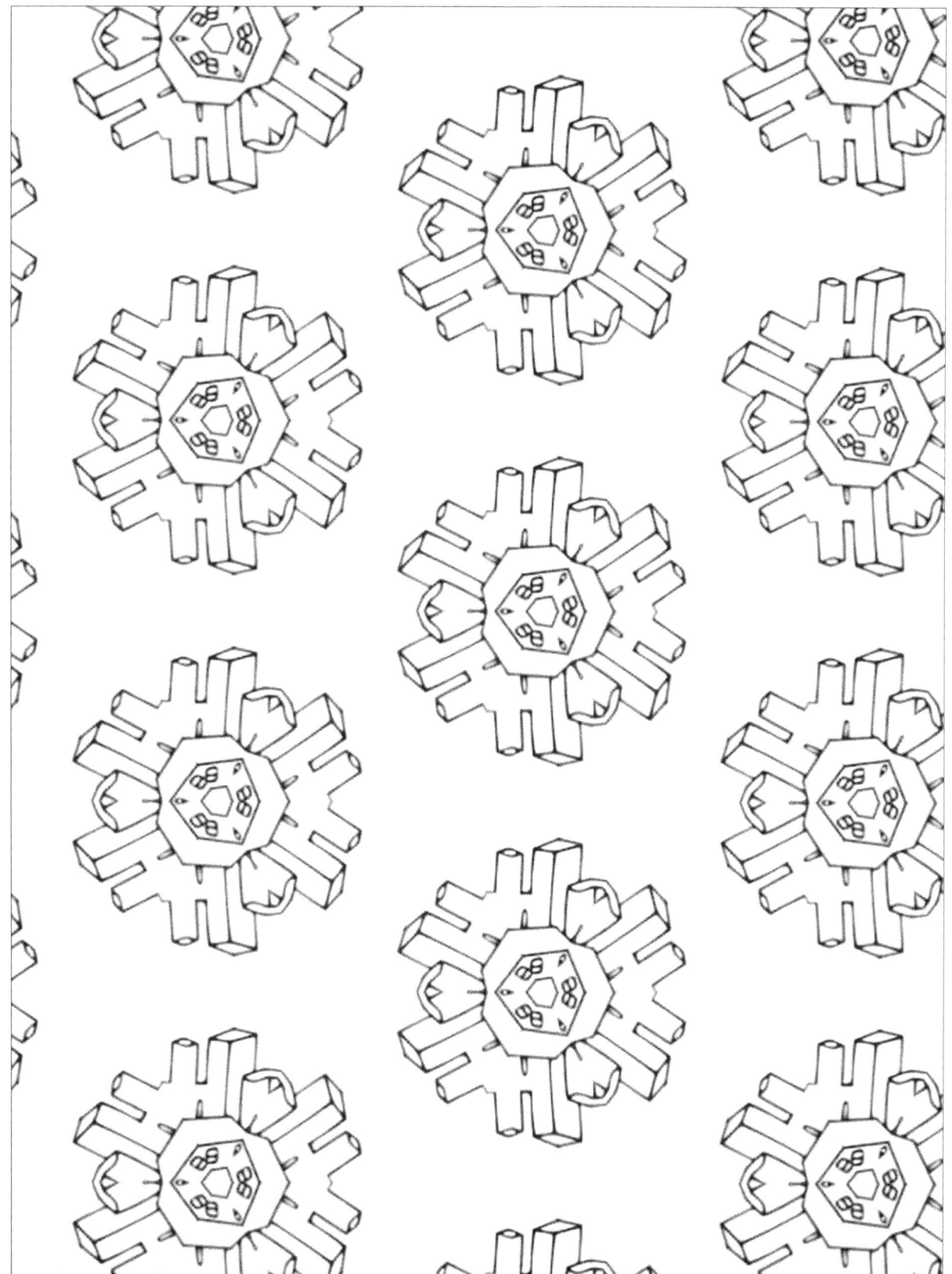

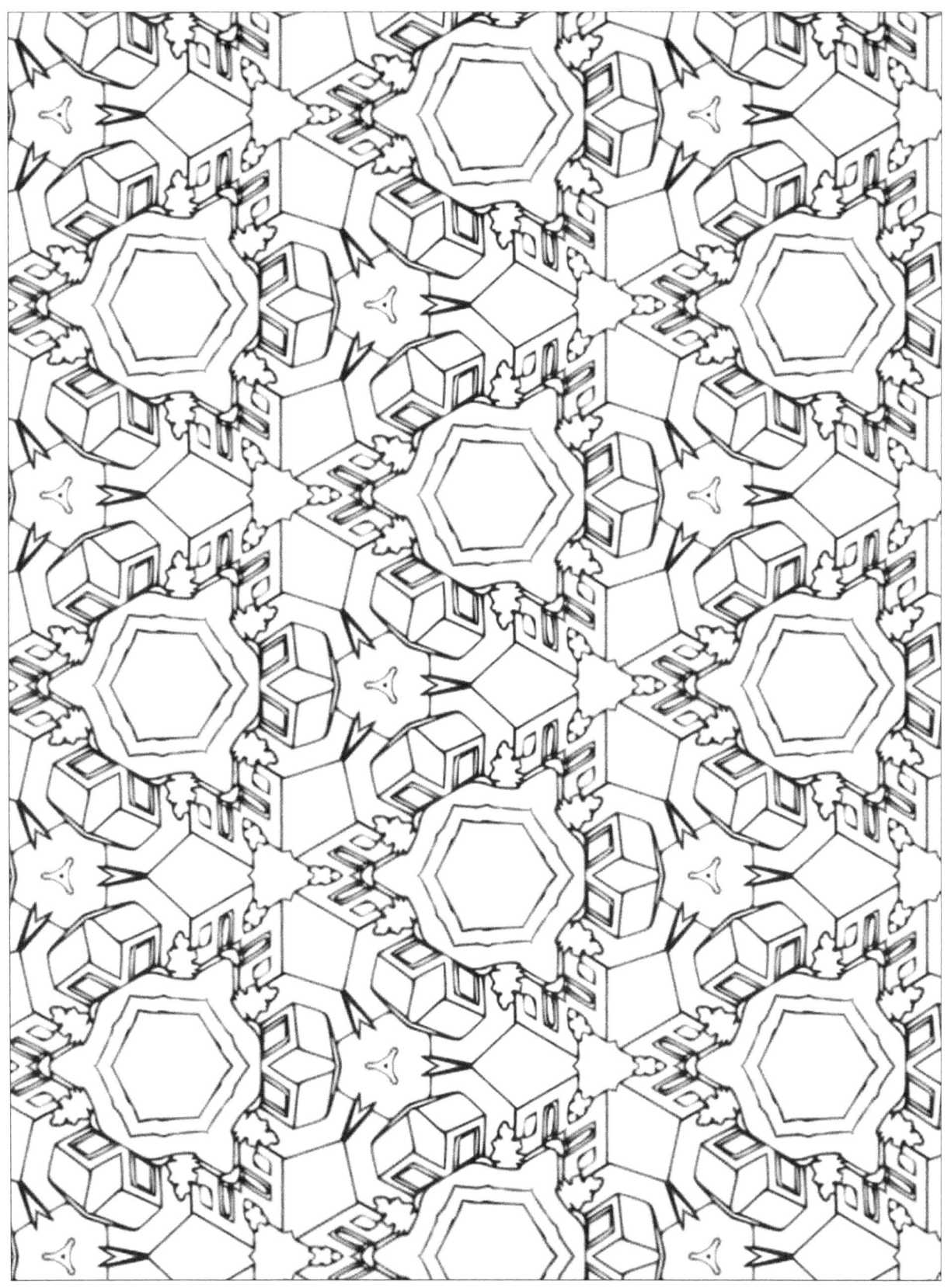

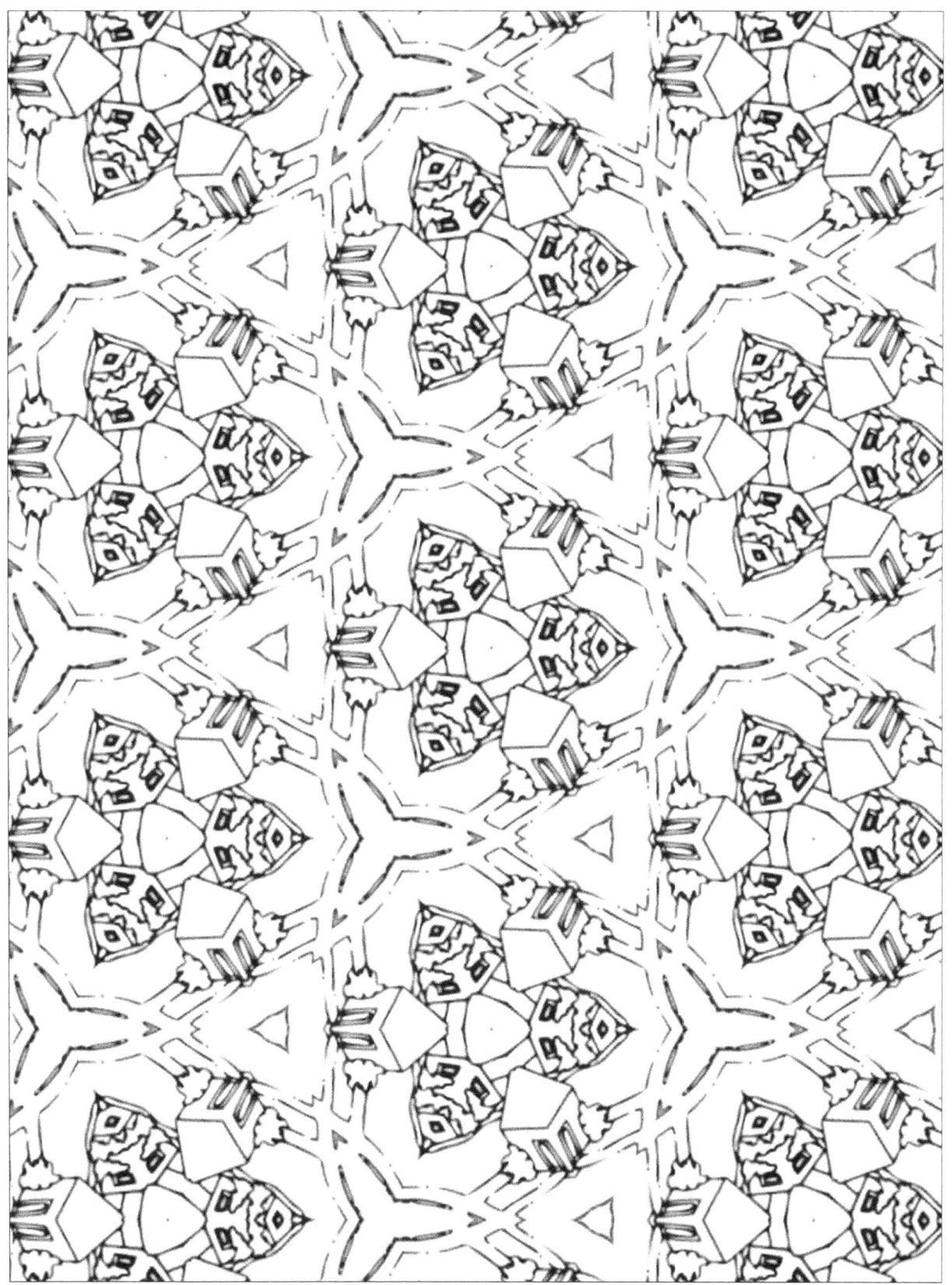

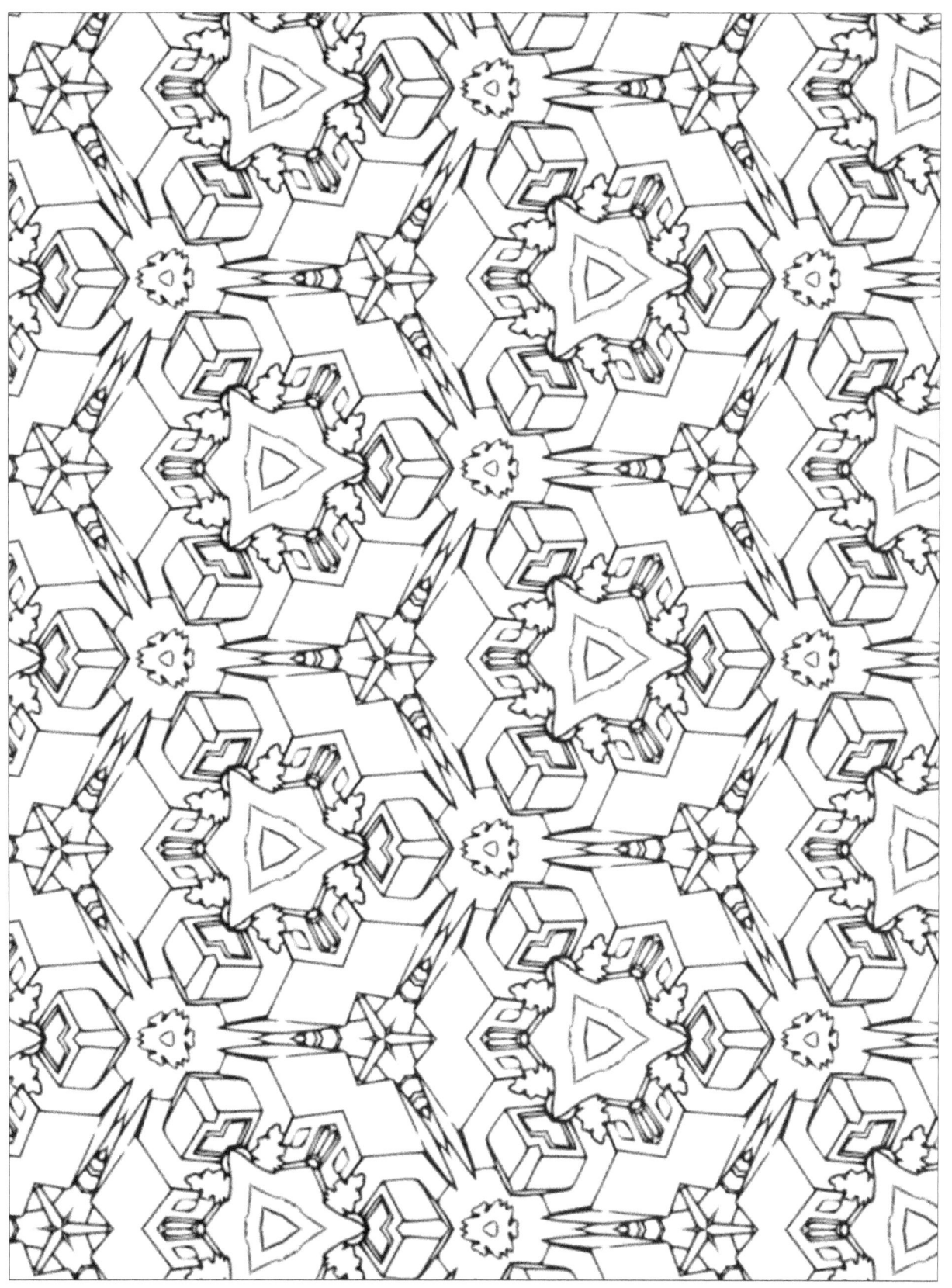

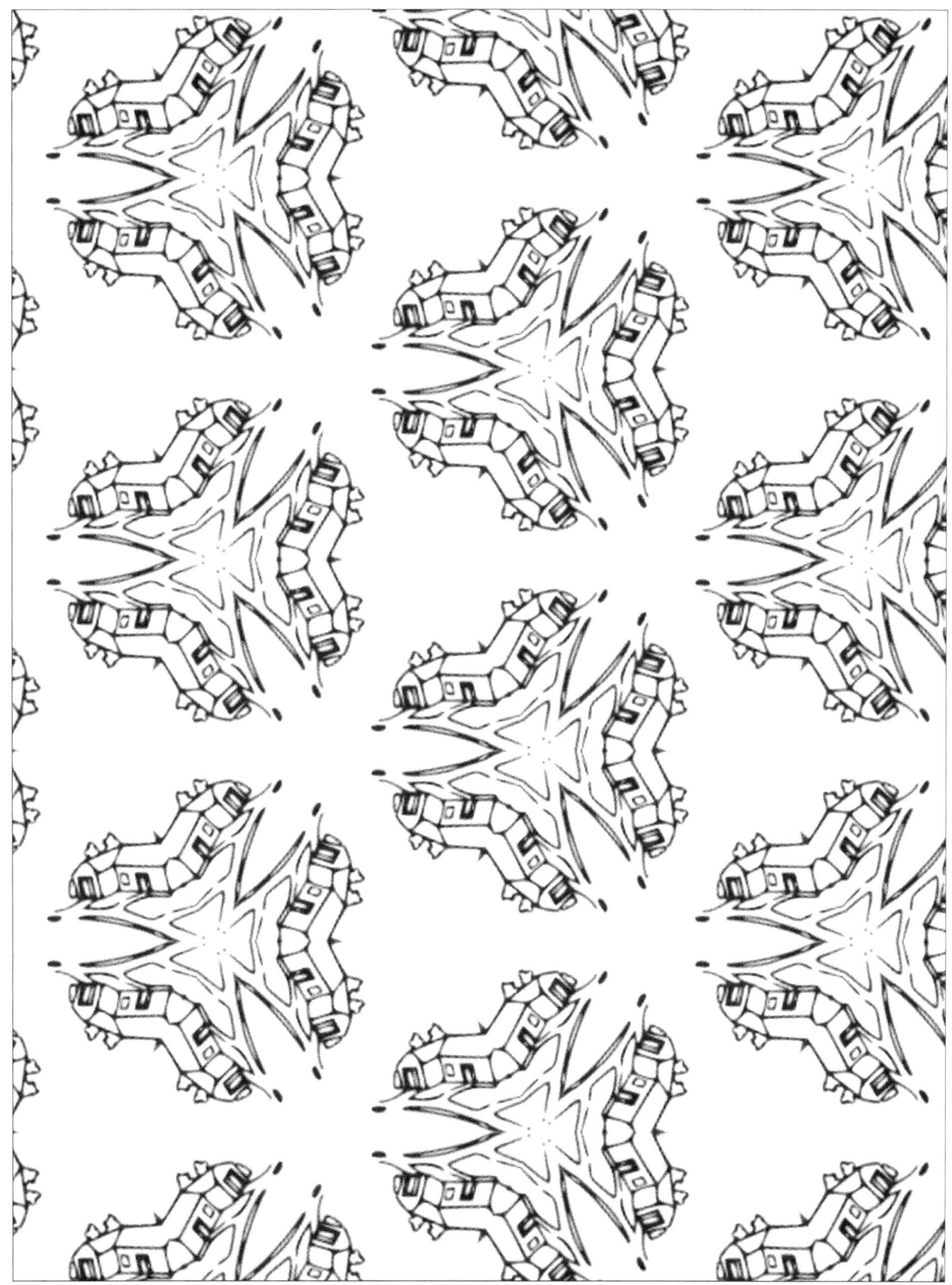

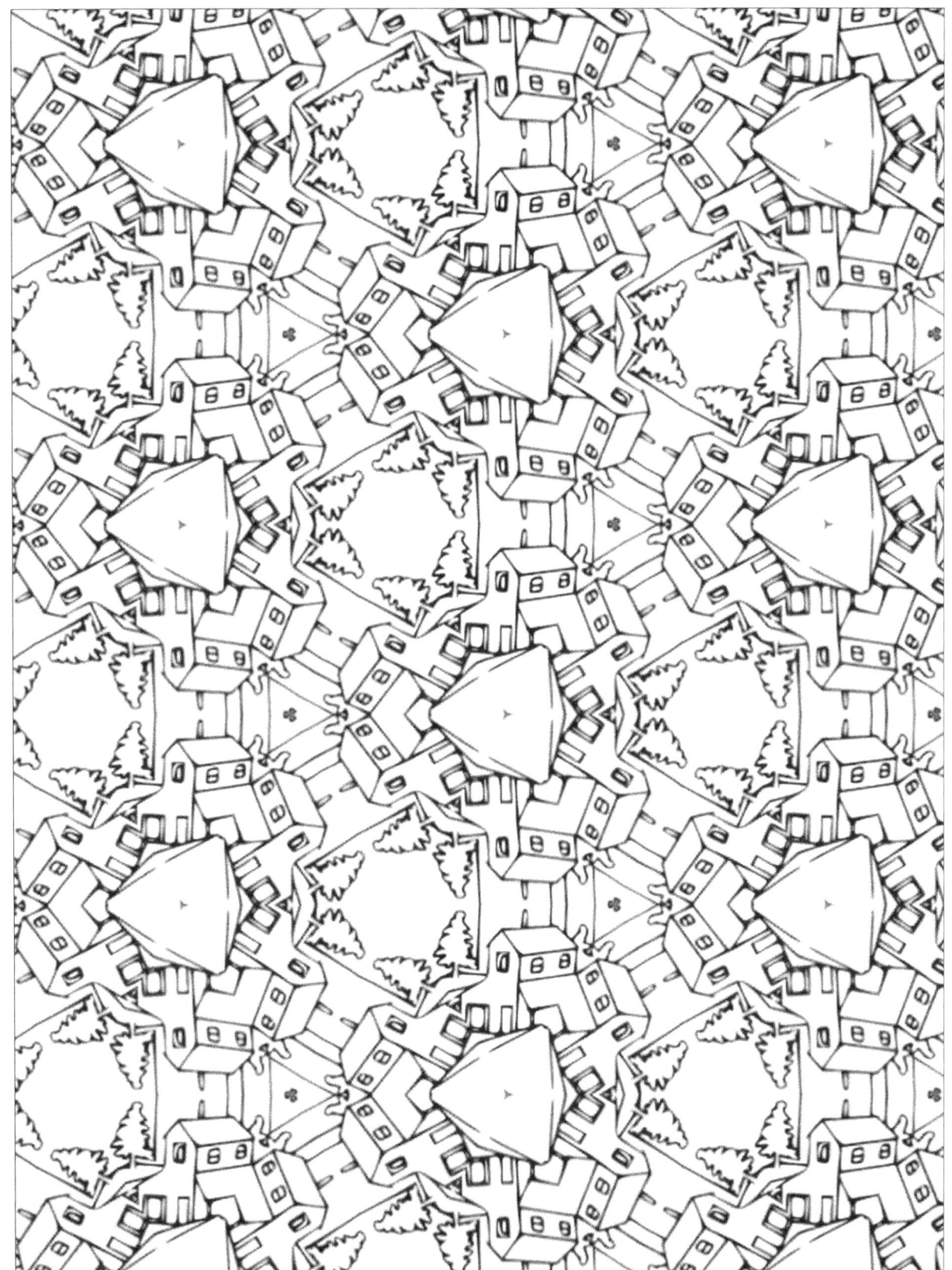

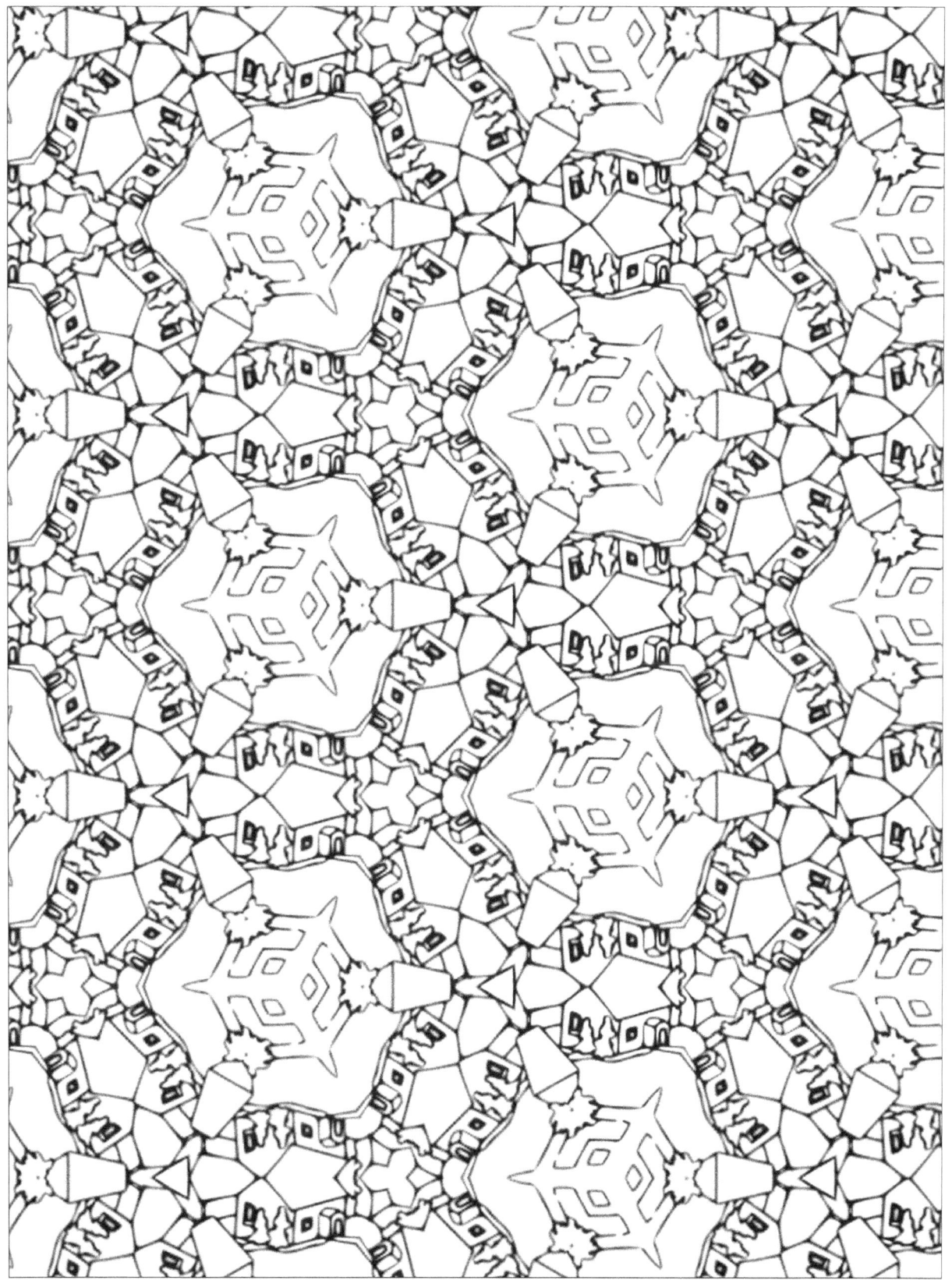

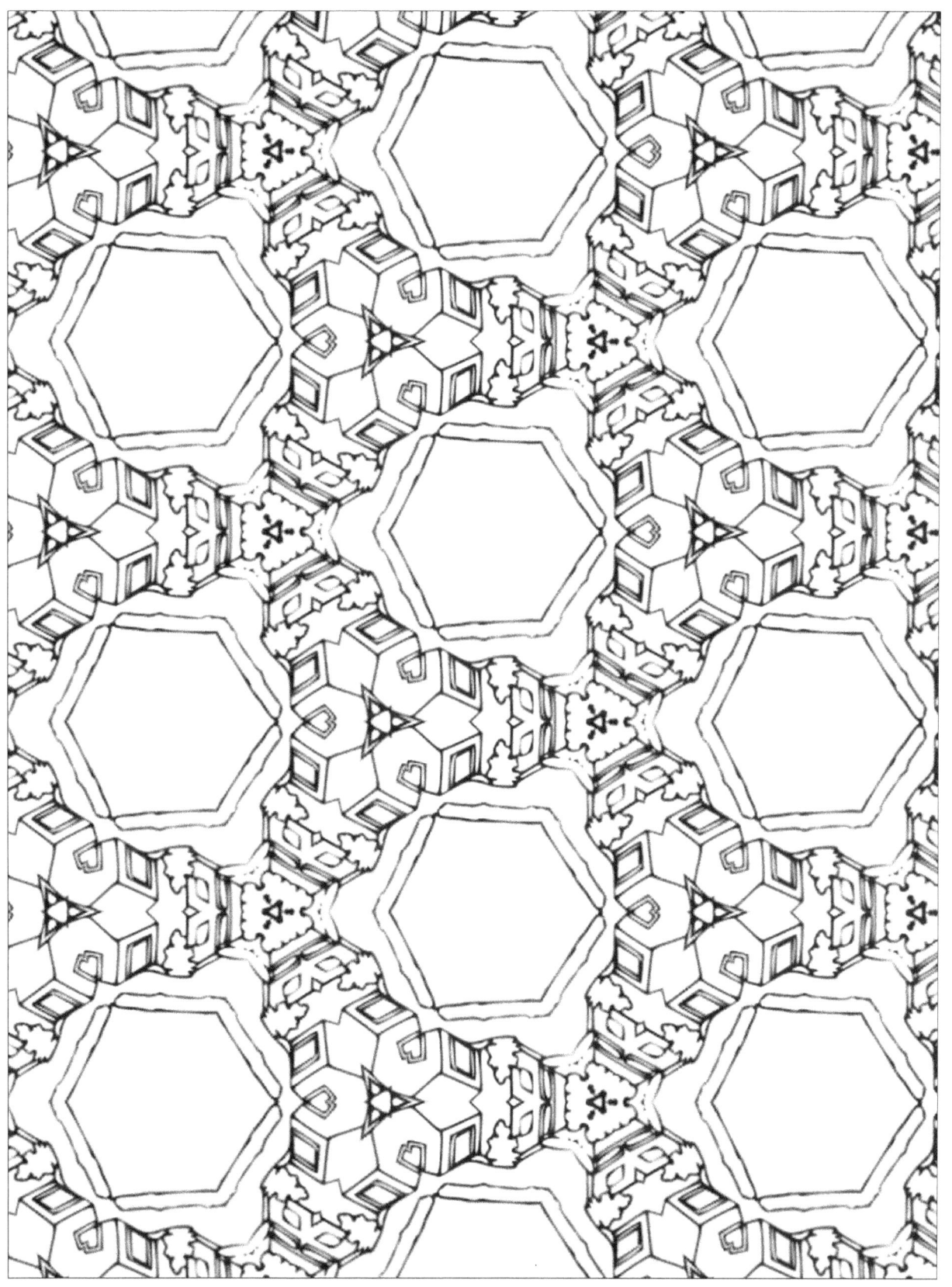

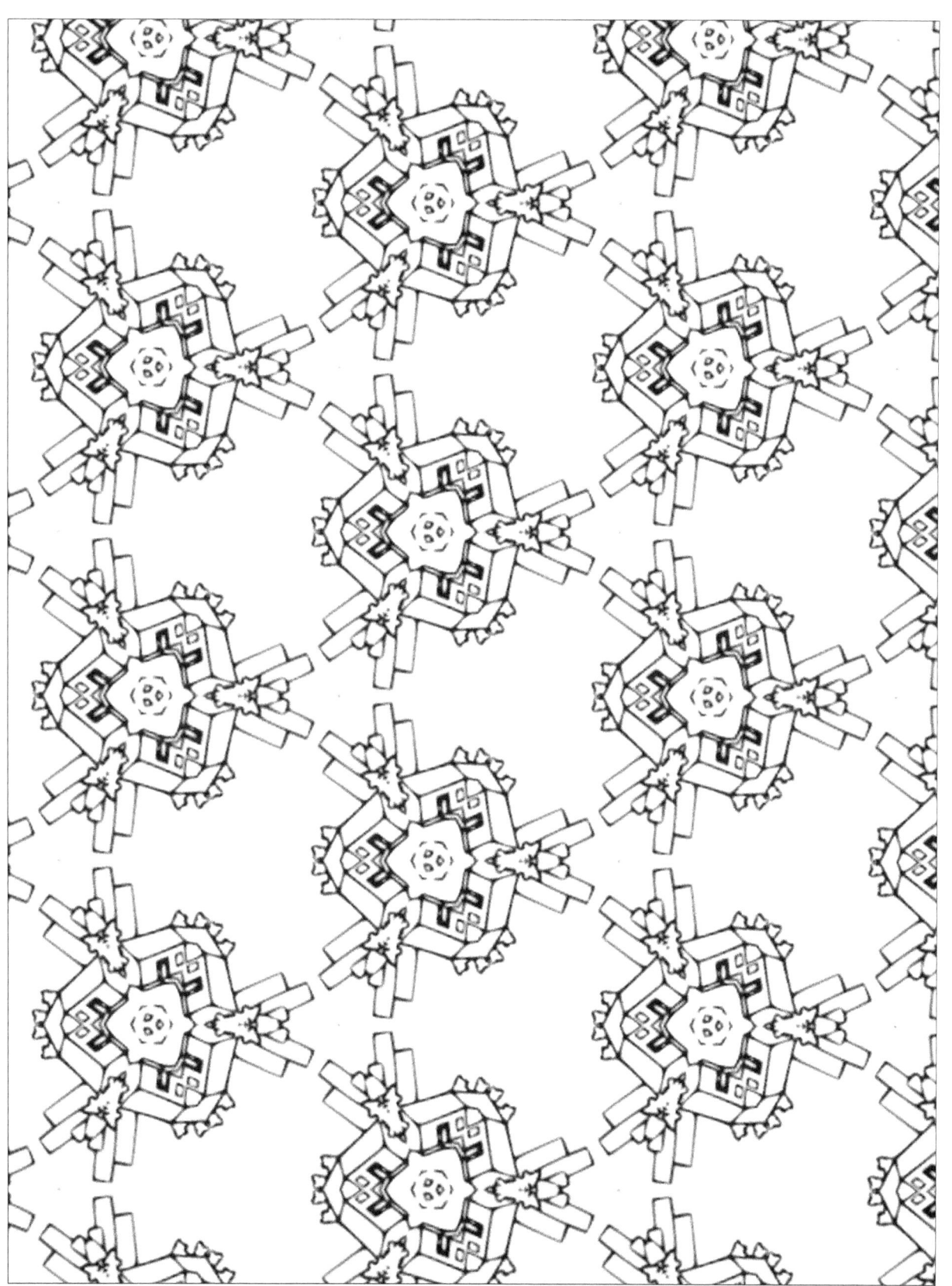

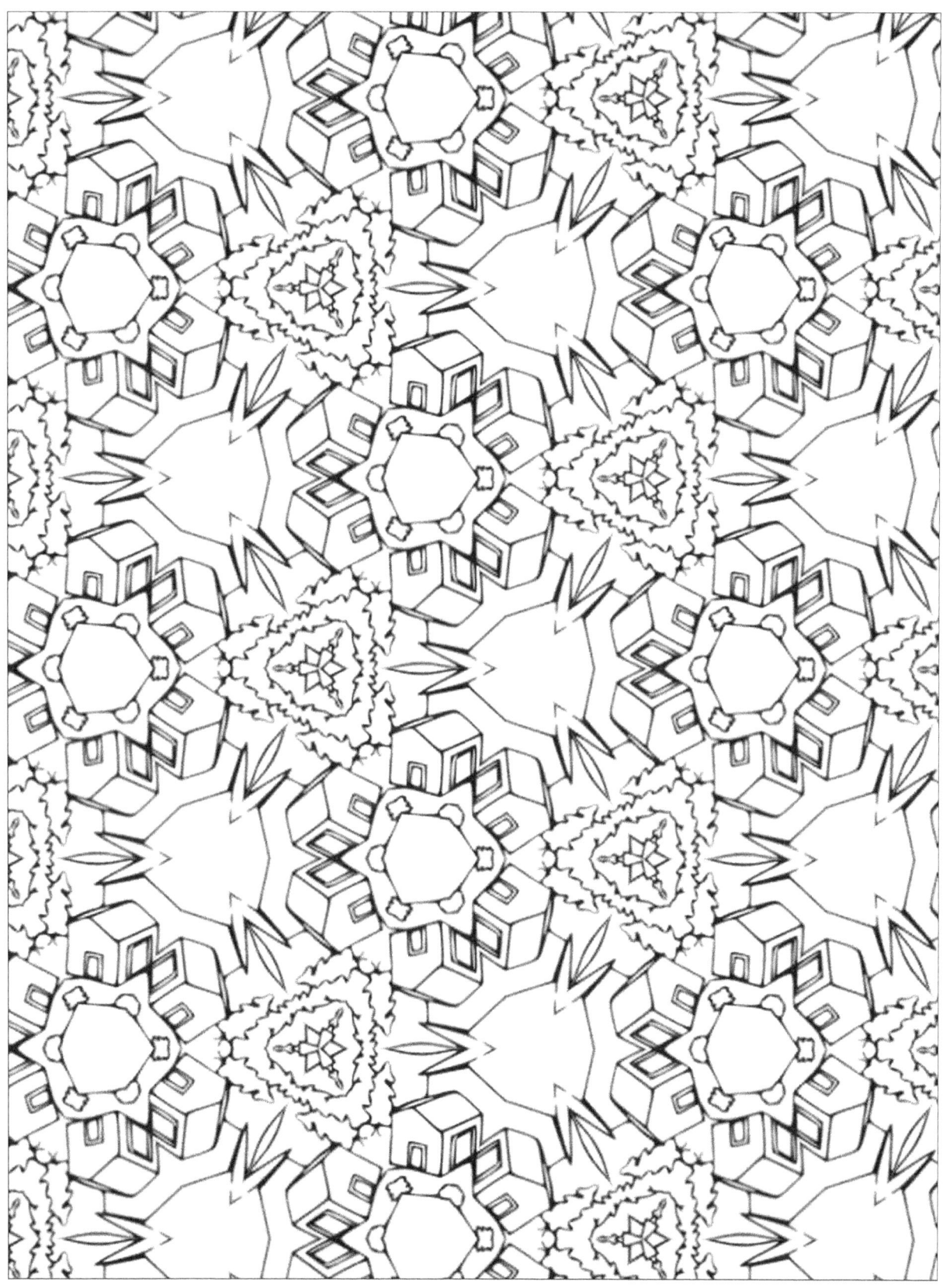

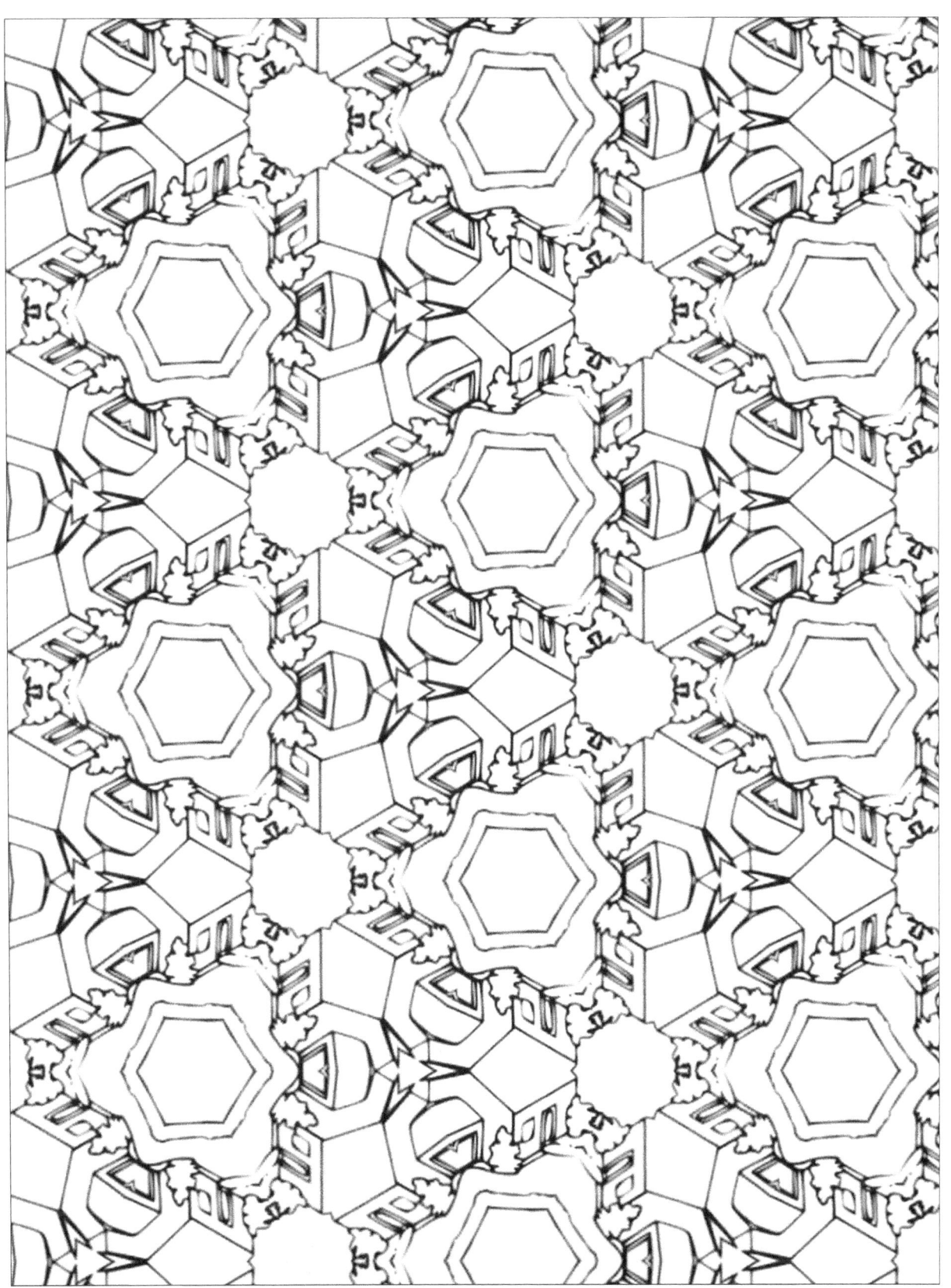

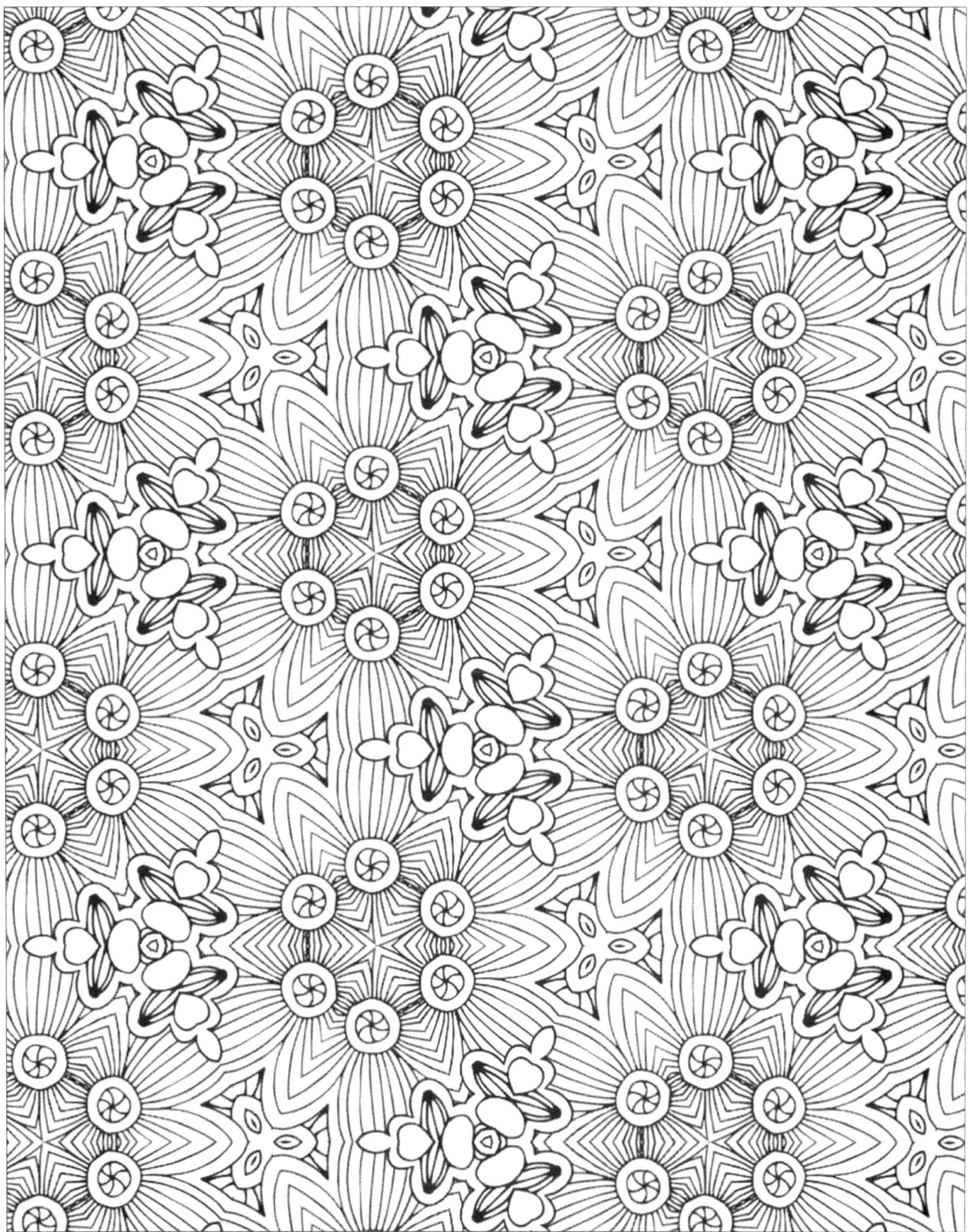

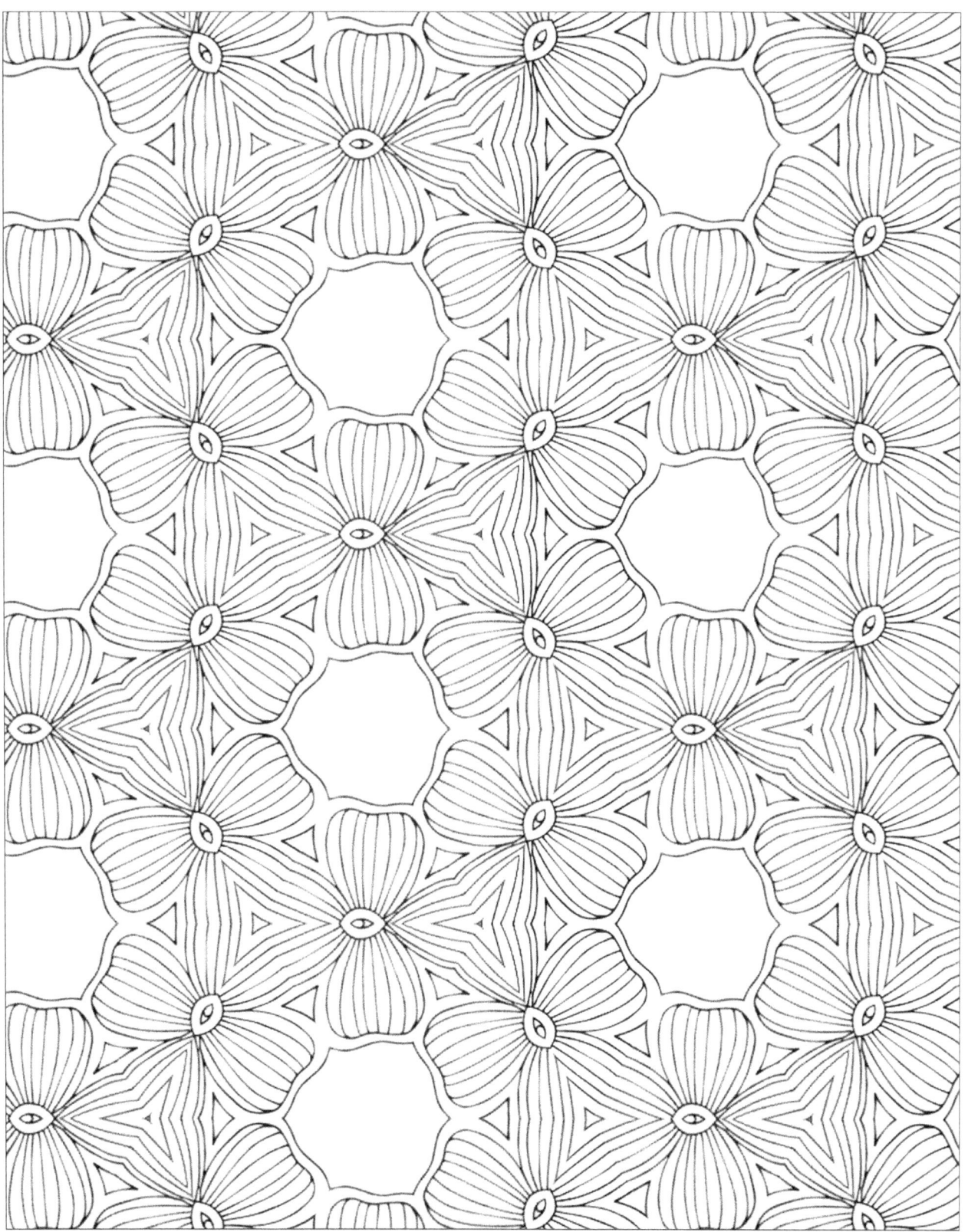

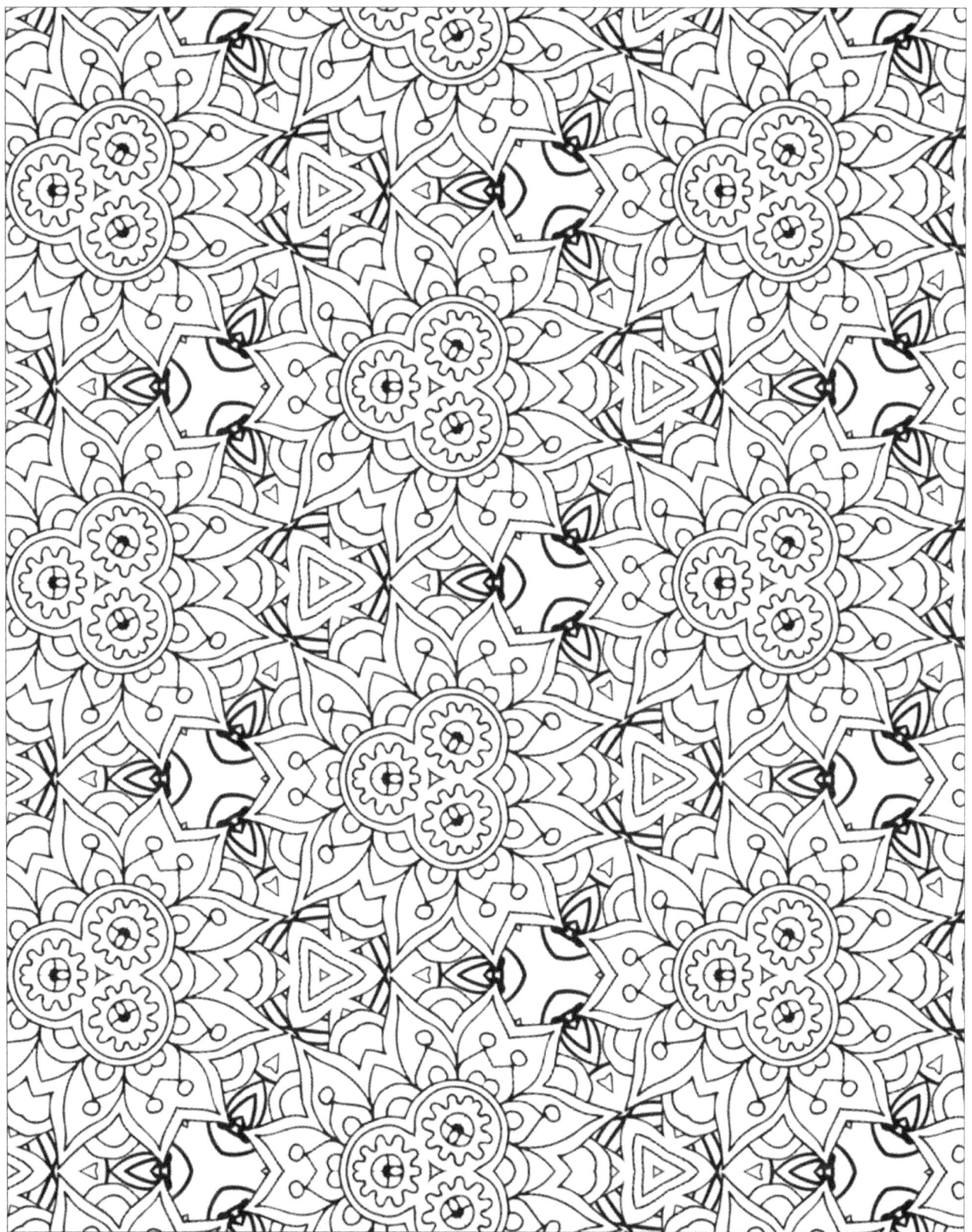

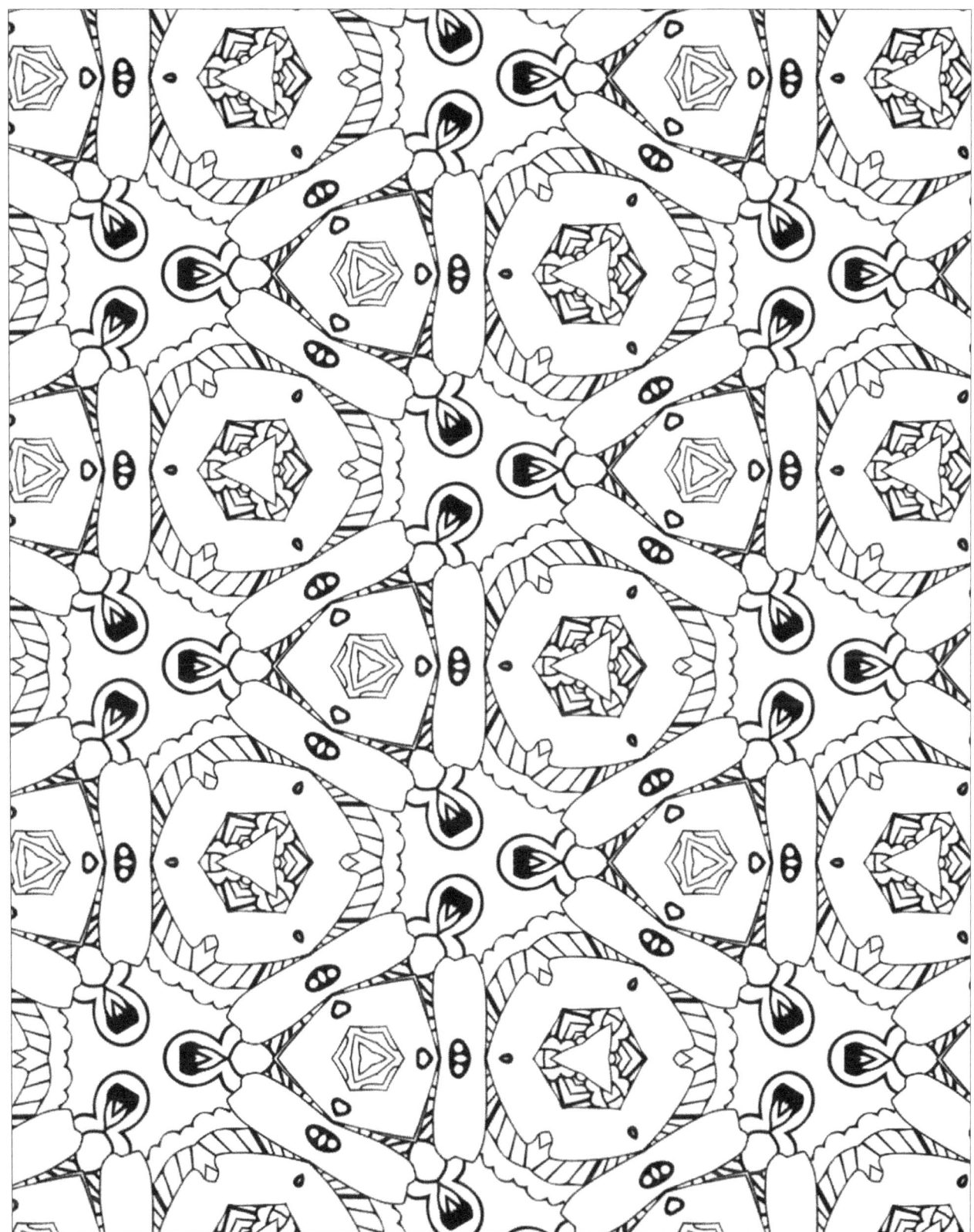

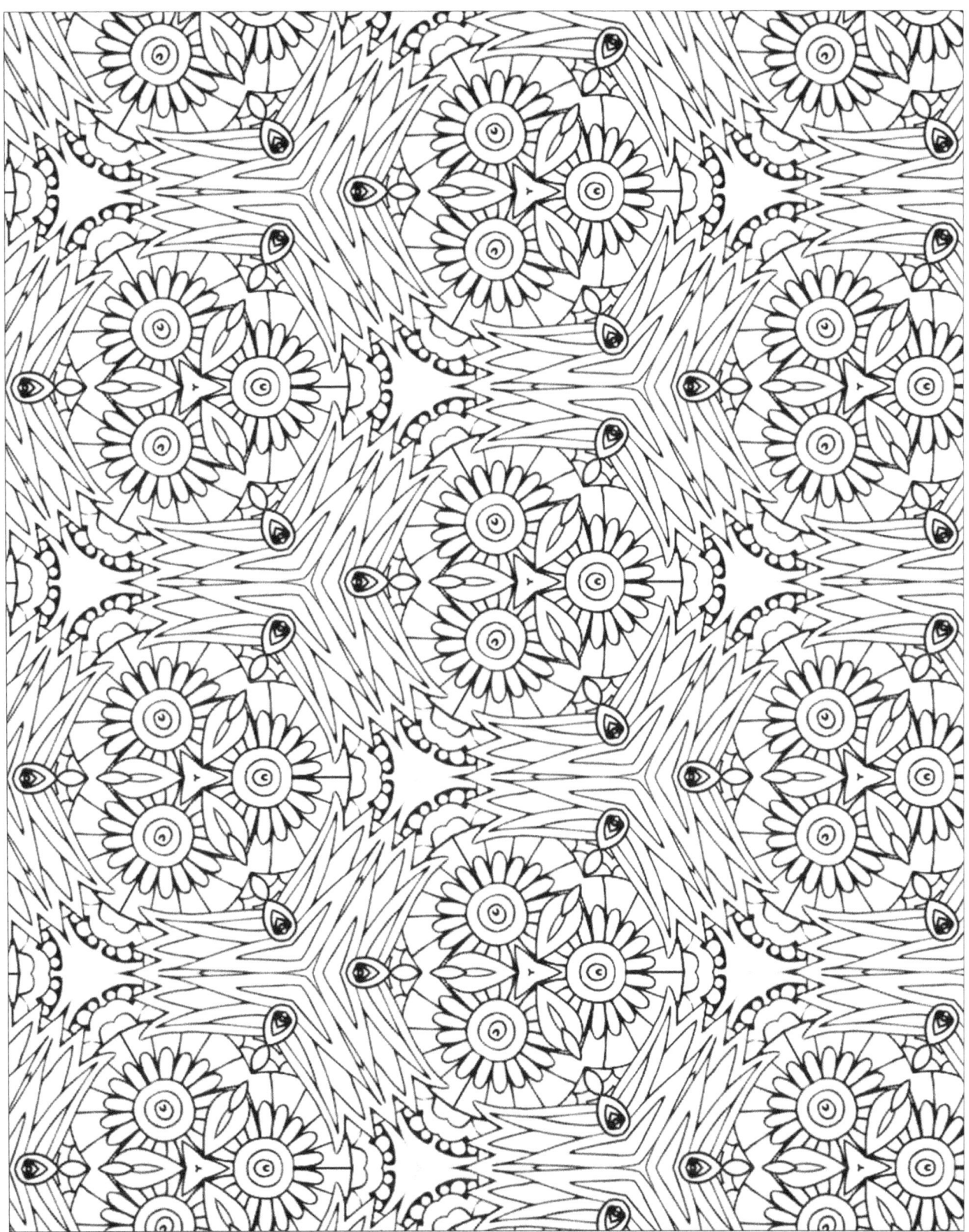

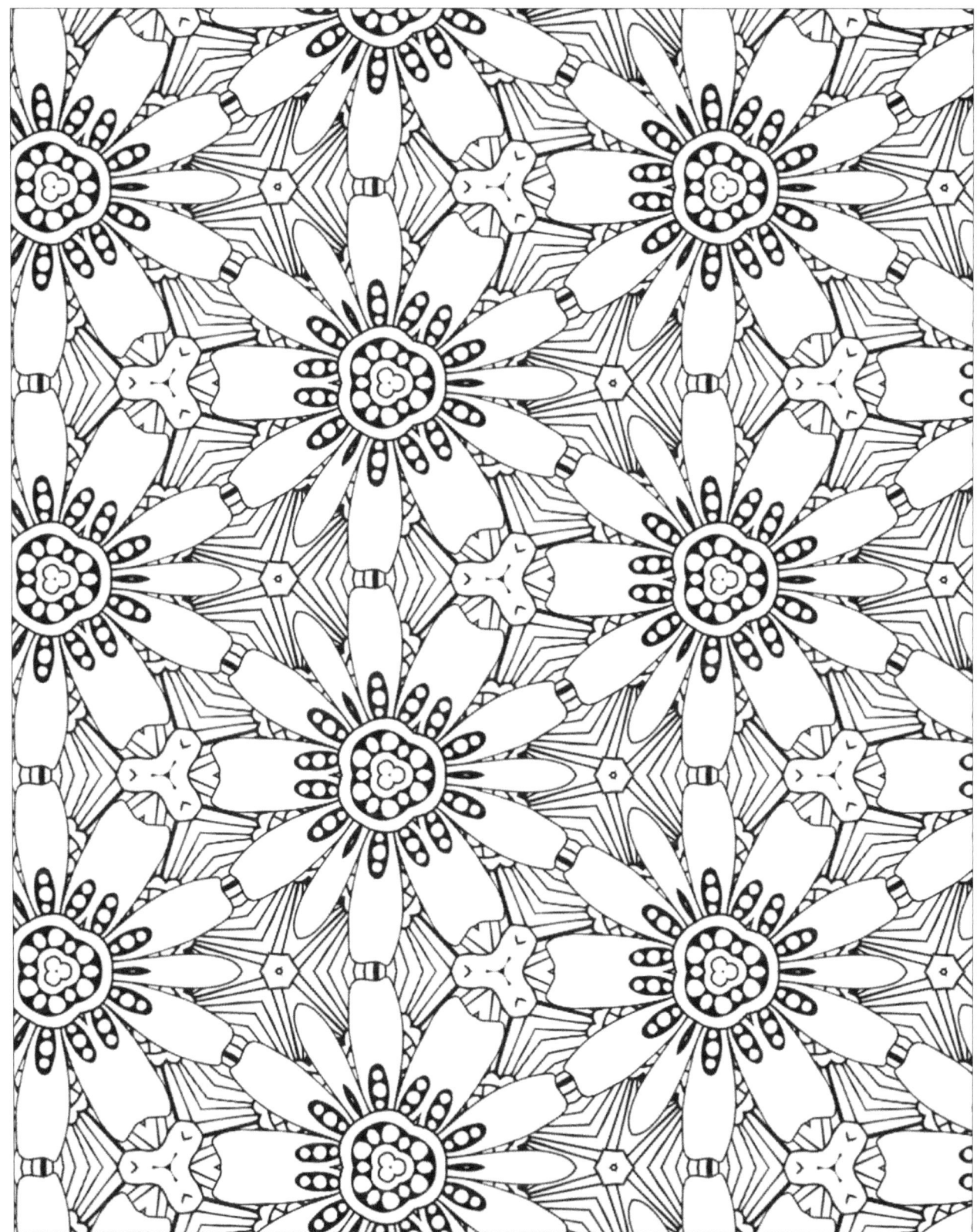

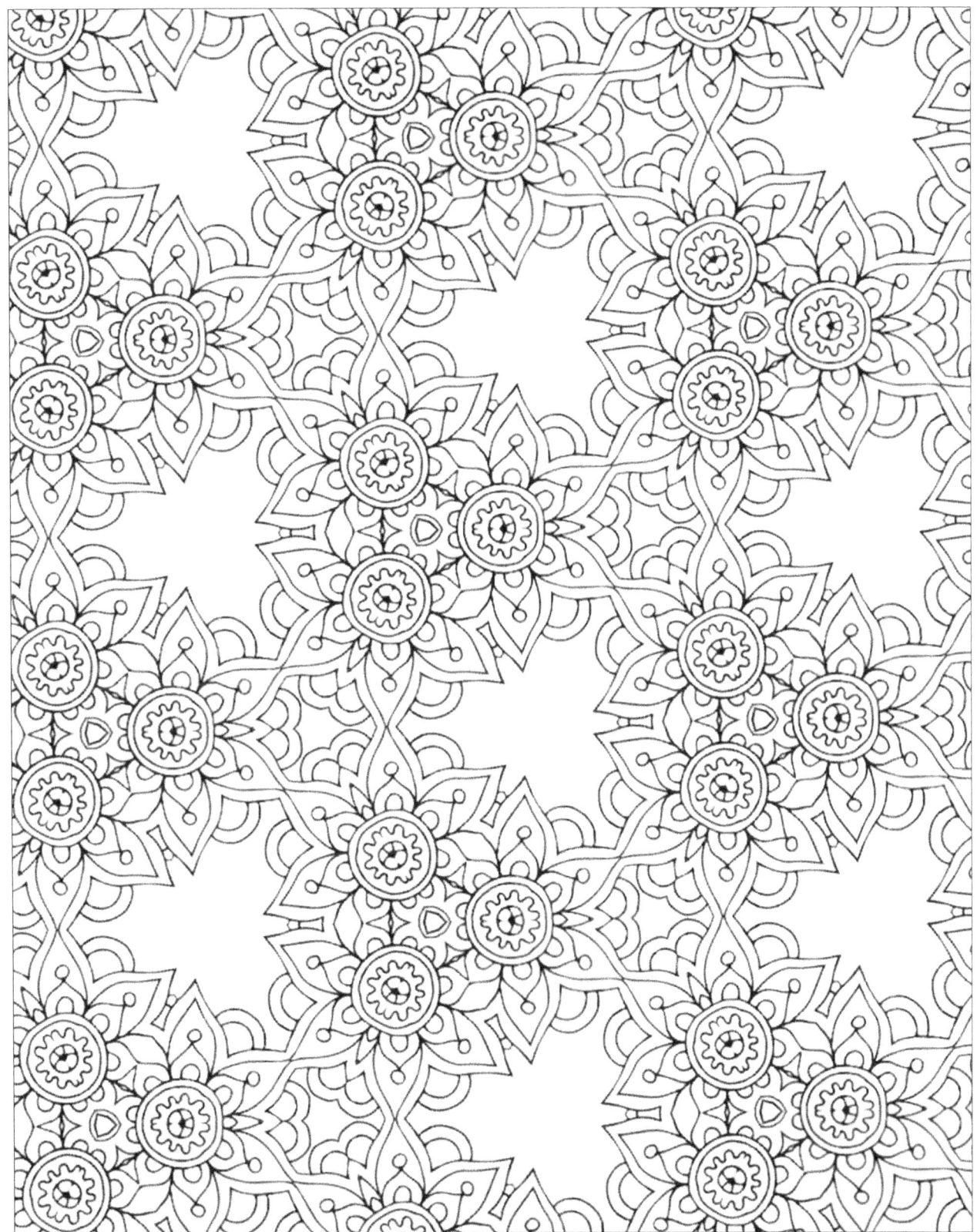

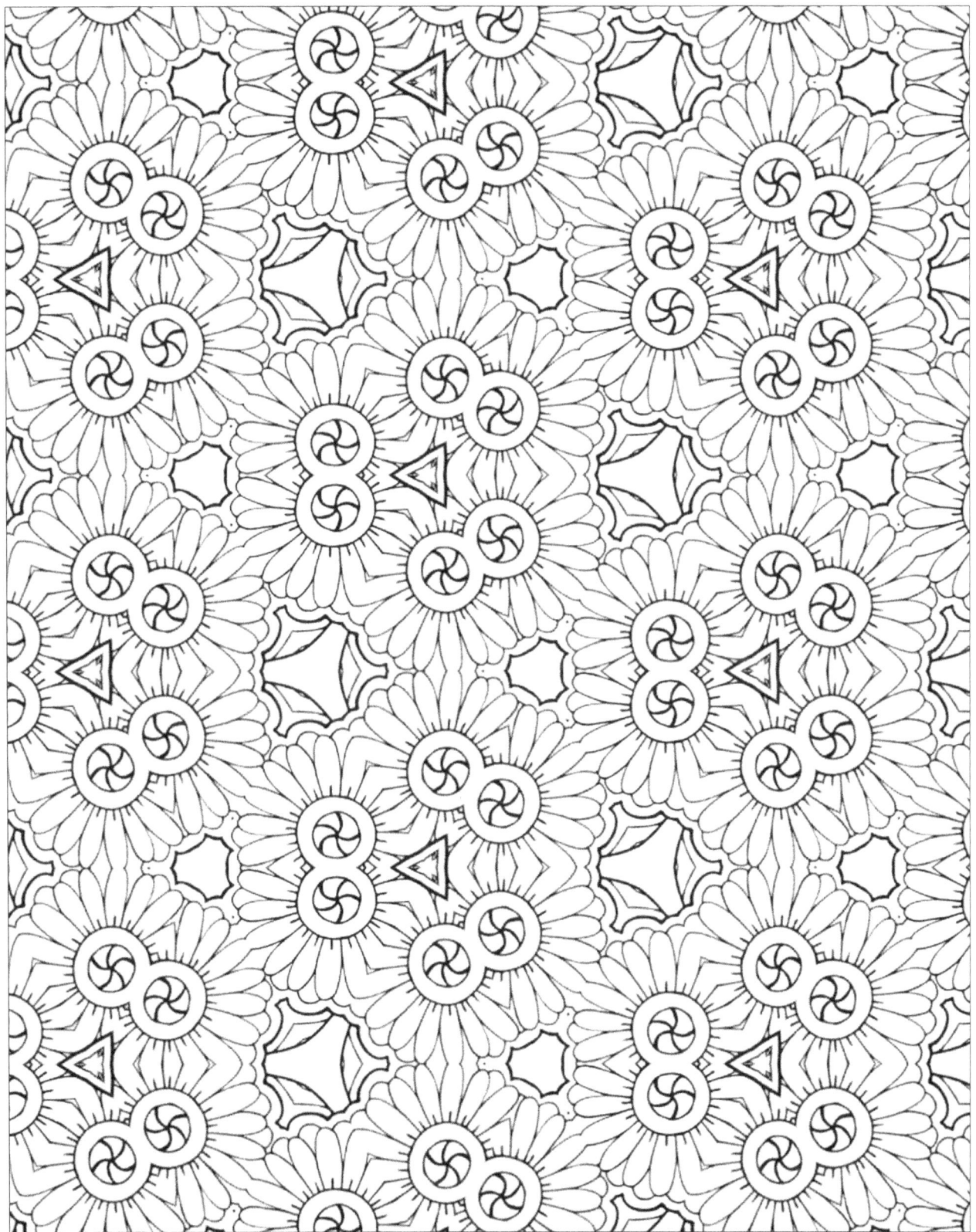

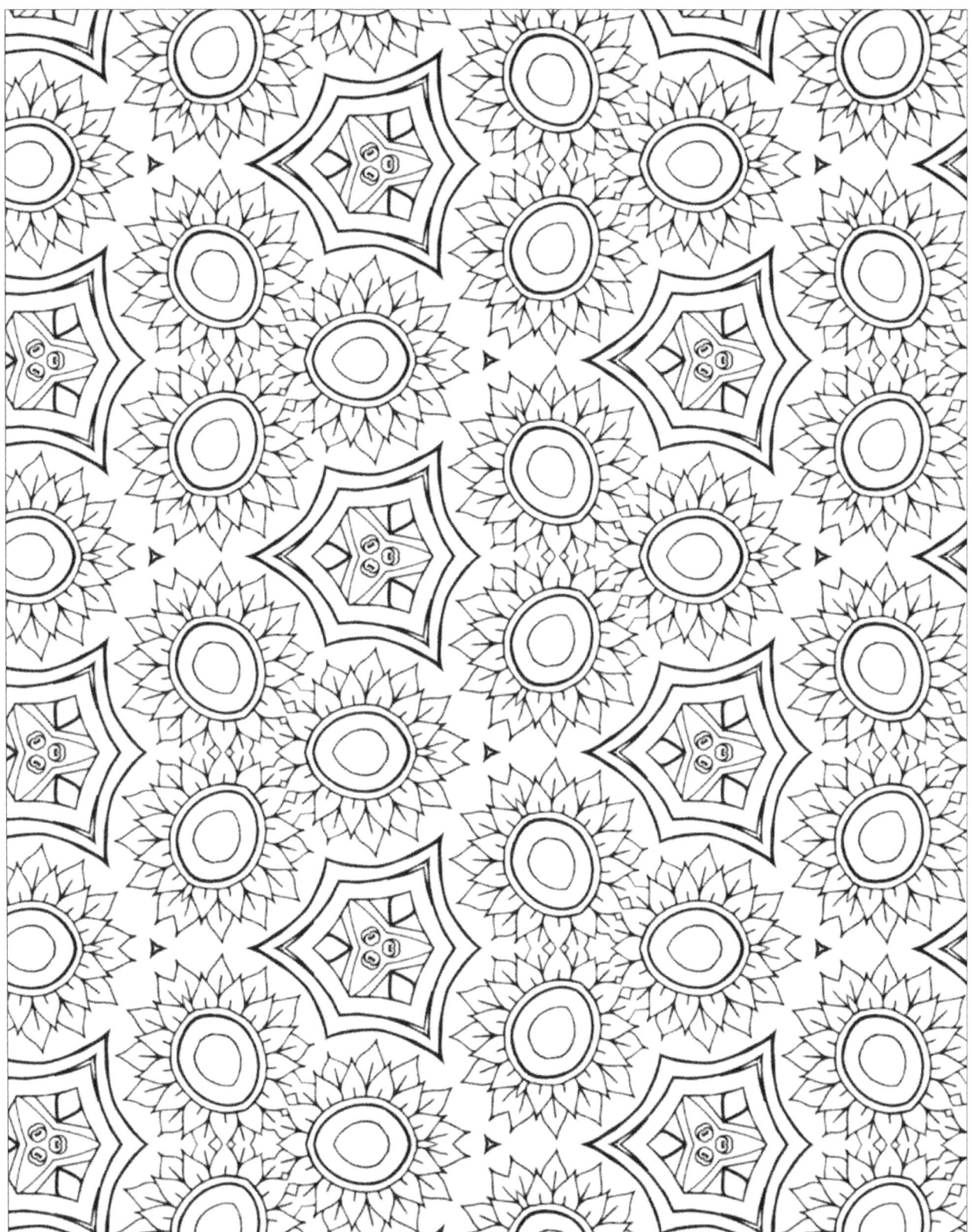

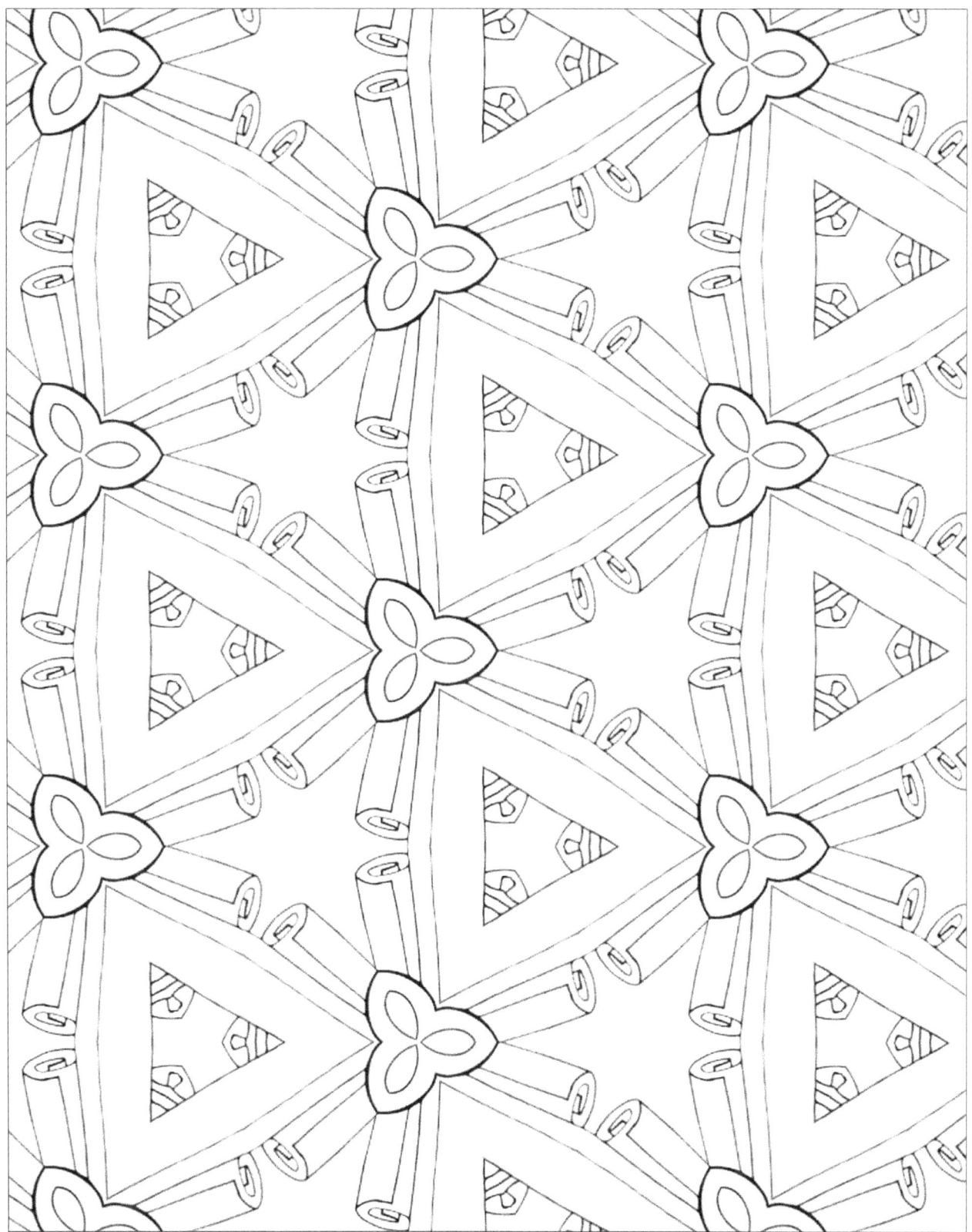

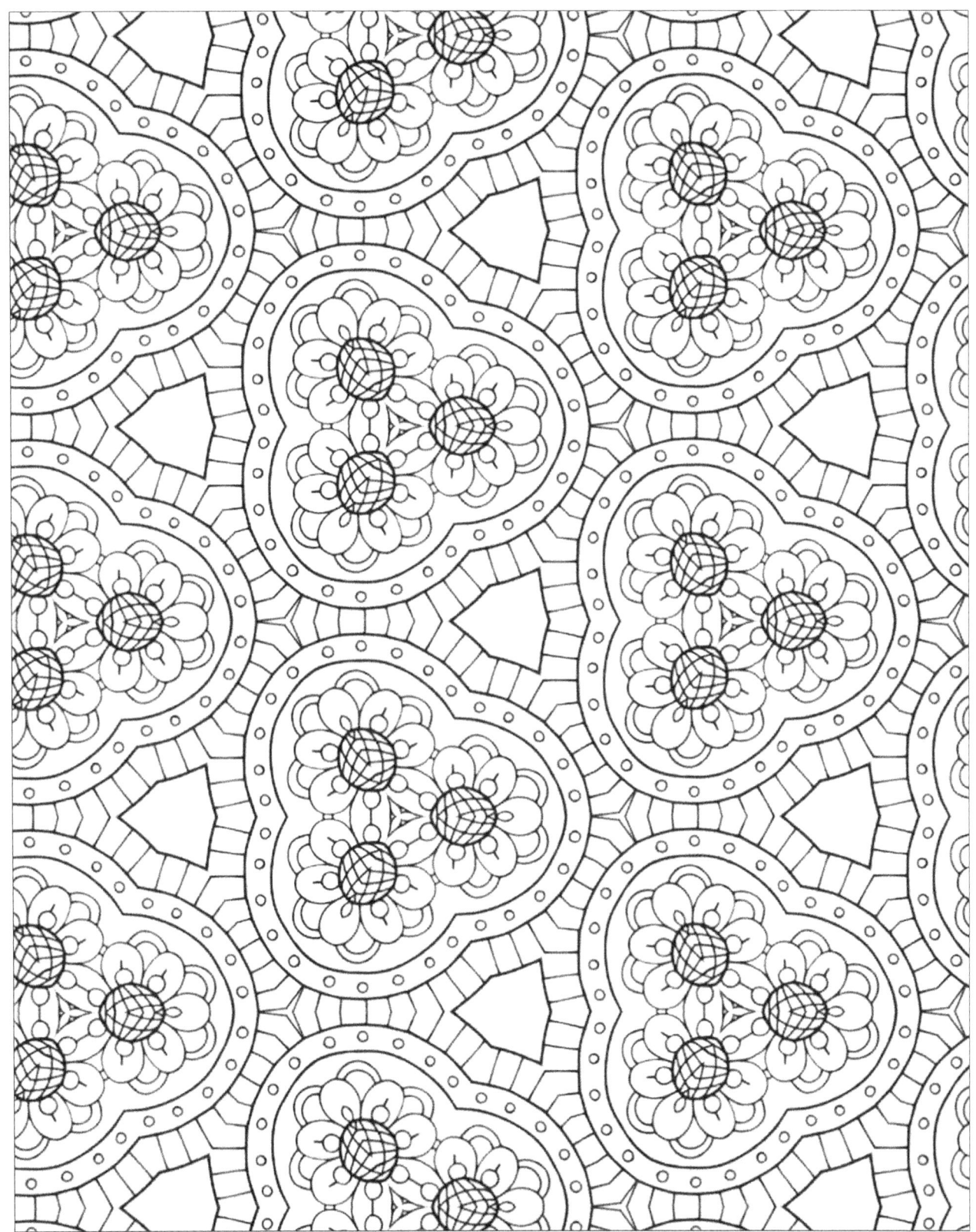

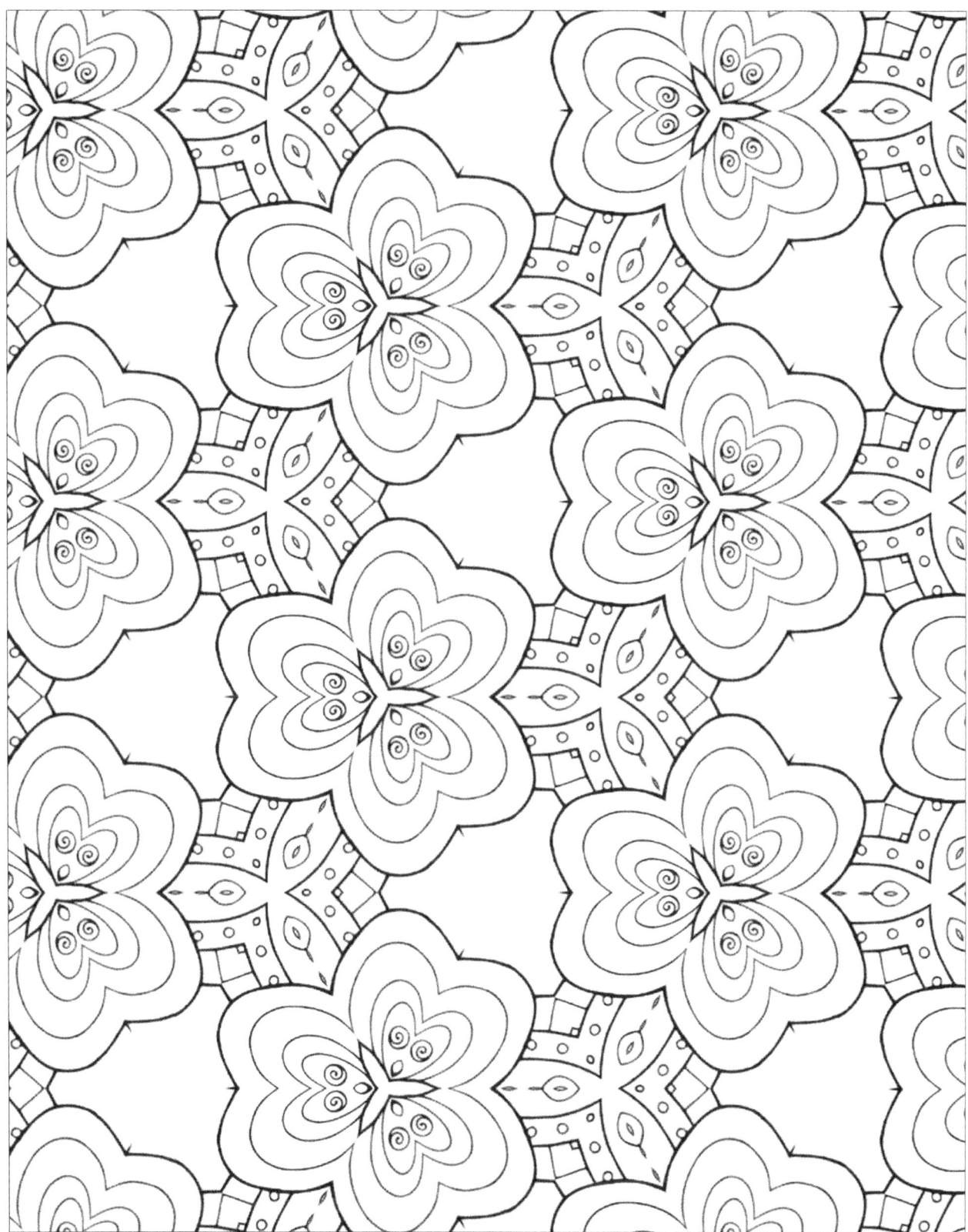

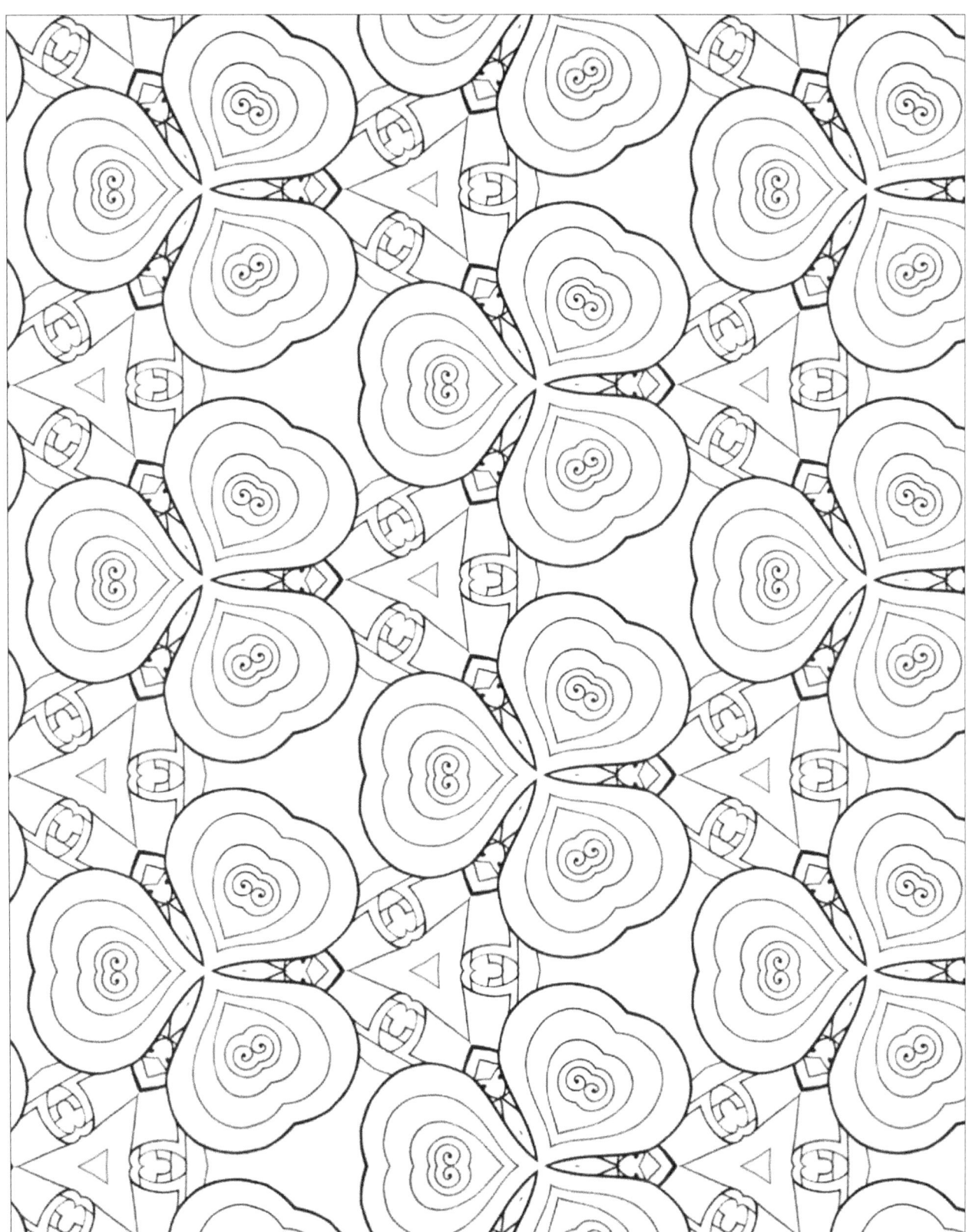

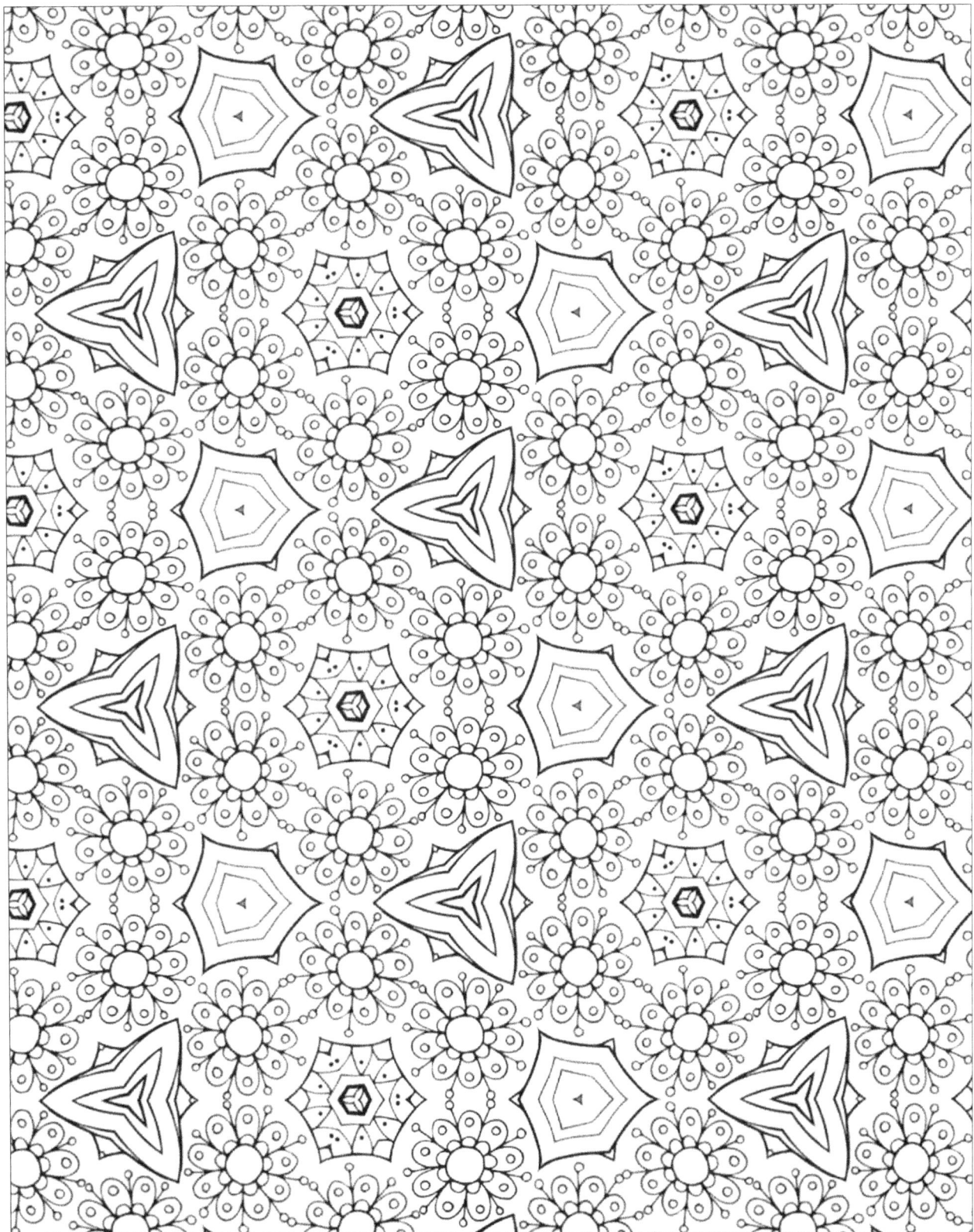

www.ingramcontent.com/pod-product-compliance
Lightning Source LLC
Chambersburg PA
CBHW080649180526
45168CB00008B/3352